CENTENNIAL   PRESS

BLUFF YOUR WAY IN WINE

Alan Fulmer
Harry Eyres

CENTENNIAL PRESS

ISBN 0-8220-2228-1
© Copyright 1990 by Centennial Press
British edition © Copyright 1987 by The Bluffer's Guides

Printed in U.S.A.
All Rights Reserved

Centennial Press, Box 82087, Lincoln, Nebraska 68501
an imprint of Cliffs Notes, Inc.

INTRODUCTION

The Mystique

Even people who are otherwise perfectly competent, who can manage to learn anything from Swahili to hydroponics to nuclear physics, are intimidated by the hallowed, rarified mystique that is inherent in the word "wine." But *you* don't have to be. After you wend your way through this book, you'll discover that to appreciate good wine, you don't have to

(1) travel extensively in Europe
(2) be a member of an exclusive country club
(3) have a wine cellar (not merely a rack in the kitchen)
(4) be able to identify *precisely* where a wine comes from without consulting the label

All you really need to know in order to bluff your way around so-called wine connoisseurs is an interest in wine and a few bucks. Supermarkets and liquor stores stock everything from rotgut to the good stuff. Don't think good wine is found only in those oak-beamed "speciality" stores—you know, the ones with the cascading cornucopias of dusty green grapes in the window. Luckily for the novice wine bluffer, the emergence of new wine countries has helped dispel part of the formidable, ridiculous mystique about wine. No longer can a "wine critic" be patronizing about anything that doesn't come from France or Germany. Non-European regions like California and Australia are now rooted firmly on the once-select vineyard map. Even *sista* and *sonnellino* lands like Spain and Italy are waking up, and unlikely countries like Bulgaria and England are surprising everybody with the quality of their wines.

But while you shouldn't be intimidated by "mystique," you should have *some* knowledge of the old traditions and etiquette so that you can challenge the wine snob at his own game and win. But watch your step. Know the places and circumstances in which you are most likely to encounter (a) wine and (b) a so-called wine expert, so that after you finish this book, you'll have both a vocabulary *and* a handful of evasive techniques that will minimize the risk of your blowing your bluff.

THE BASICS

What Is Wine?

The answer is 100-proof idiot-proof. Wine is fermented grape juice. Period. Sure, old grannies of both sexes and their apprentices make, drink, and even talk ad nauseam about elderberry wine, peach wine, dandelion wine, or whatever, but forget that crowd, and, above all, avoid accepting (in public) Aunt Martha's annual gift of her Mason-Jar-Fumé. These wines have absolutely *no* mystique, no bluffing potential. Non-alcoholic wines aren't wines. Wines, like some human beings, need to be alcoholic.

The Three Colors

The color of a wine is the result of the length of time the skins remain with the juice during the fermentation process. That's fairly easy to remember, and basically, wine comes in three colors:

(1) **Reds** (reddish-purple to light brown)
(2) **Whites** (whitish, pale yellow to amber)
(3) **Blushes** (peach to light pink)

Never, but *never* utter the word "rosé."

Sweet and Dry

All wines (well, practically all of them) are naturally dry. "Sweetness" occurs when the fermentation is interrupted before all the sugar is converted to alcohol. The producer can also add unfermented grape juice or sugar, usually in liquid form. Not real kosher, but it happens.

Don't jump to the conclusion, though, that you should turn thumbs down on sweet wines. Only ignorant yokels ridicule sweet wines; they've done it for years. Therefore, you can score a winning bluff by praising the little-known sweet white wines of the Loire Valley or the really fine German Auslese, Beerenauslese, and Trockenbeerenauslese wines. Don't bother clogging your glottal stops with the last two — shorten them to BA and TBA, and if you want to ruffle the feathers of some preeningly snooty wine peacock, recommend an Austrian TBA from a place called Rust (pronounced "roost").

Fortification

Most wines are *un*fortified. In other words, they contain only the alcohol that God provided — in the marriage of sun and grapes (or perhaps sugar beets if the wine's French). However, some wines — like port, sherry, Madeira, and those two has-beens Marsala and Malaga — are strengthened by the addition of everything from brandy to industrial alcohol. Fortified wines, like a woman scorned, aren't to be taken lightly. They get you buzzing in 20 minutes and can leave you with a two-day hangover if you aren't careful.

Still and Sparkling

Sparkling wines are bottled in either thick, heavy-set bottles with wire-bound corks (which take longer to remove than to drink the entire bottle). Still wines are bottled in ordinary bottles with ordinary corks (usually impossible to get out). Simple, right? Not really; there's one small problem with still wines. Many of them are slightly fizzy (sorry, "sparkling"). Sometimes this is intentional, as with the Portuguese Vinho Verde. But even when it's not intentional, it isn't necessarily bad. So, if you're served a *slightly* sparkling still wine, say, "Hmmm . . . slightly *pétillant*" (if it's French) or "Hmmm . . . slightly *spritzig*" (if it's German). Problem solved.

ESSENTIAL EQUIPMENT

Nose

Ninety percent of a wine's taste is savored by the nose. Remember the last time you had a bad cold? Nothing tasted good because you couldn't *smell* it. Don José Ignacio Domecq (of the famous Spanish sherry firm) possesses the most famous nose in the wine business. His particular nose is long and thin and fits conveniently inside the small tapered sherry glasses called *copitas.* It's probably a case of natural selection. Non-sherry tasters don't need such impressive beaks, of course, but the equipment inside the schnoz must operate properly.

Cash

Good wine isn't cheap, and unless you can convince a liquor store owner that you write books (or a weekly column) about wine, you're going to have to fork over some dough to support your habit. Unlike bluffing your way in some areas, bluffing your way in wine requires special disciplines: wine has to be bought and consumed to be appreciated – especially if you're going to succeed as a good-vintaged bluffer.

Corkscrews

Forget about all wines that are sold in boxes or cans. Respectable wines come in bottles with corks – despite the fact that no one has invented a really good device for extracting corks. That's why, in the old days, hot-tempered gentlemen used to decapitate bottles with red-hot pincers. This technique is out of style today, and, anyway, it's tough to do without a blazing fire. Thus, the bluffer should probably get the so-called waiter's friend, or the "screwpull." (More about this later; first, some Don'ts.)

Corkscrews to be avoided at *all* costs include the double-armed ratchet type (which has a drill-like screw that bores holes through the cork and catches your fingers in its ratchets) and the vacuum variety which pumps the air out. With this latter kind, you can blow up the bottle and disfigure your date for life.

Go for the simplest possible kind of corkscrew – as long as it's got a good, smooth, sinuous screw and a comfortable, firmly attached handle. Stressing the importance of a proper screw can have intriguing implications – as well as the advantage of actually popping the cork.

Glasses

It's generally agreed that wine should be drunk from a glass, but for really desperate souls, any container will do. The aspiring bluffer should know that glasses have the advantage of *not* affecting flavor – unlike leather bottles, metal goblets, or old boots. With glass, you can see what you're drinking.

The glass itself is relatively unimportant, but a tulip-shaped glass, which gathers the bouquet, is considered best. The simpler the better. The bluffer should avoid cut-glass and engraved glasses, fluted glasses (which let the bouquet escape), and, above all, the extra-large, balloon-shaped glasses. They're ostentatious and have all kinds of undesirable connotations.

Decanters

They're very distinquished looking and very impressive sitting on the sideboard, but they're really unnecessary—except for very old red wines and vintage and crusted ports which have vile-looking sediment in the bottom of the bottles; as far as brandy is concerned, no one can decide whether or not to decant (so, if you *have* a decanter, decant it). Decanting, apart from separating the wine from the sediment, exposes wine to the atmosphere and lets it "breathe." Some wines, however, especially very old ones, don't appreciate the atmosphere and fade away like aging southern belles. Decanting very old wines is risky business. As are aging southern belles.

White wines (sherry included) should *not* be decanted. Ever. It's unnecessary and it's harmful to the wine; besides, the result will seem unpleasantly medicinal (perhaps one reason white wine is usually sold in green bottles). As for cheap port, you can decant it if you want to; you can also pass it off as vintage. Go for it.

Decanting-Made-Easy is the process of pouring all the contents of the bottle into a decanter and stopping the pouring *just before* the "solids" get in. It sounds easy and it *is* easy. But you've got to make it *look* difficult.

If possible, orchestrate your performance to resemble a Black Mass. Light a candle and set it underneath the bottle being poured (supposedly to show when the sediment reaches the neck, but in fact to conjure ceremonial atmosphere). Maintain absolute silence and a look of deep concentration until you've transferred the very last drop of clear liquid. Afterward, emit a dramatic sigh, wipe your brow theatrically, and momentarily feign emotional exhaustion. (Imagine Richard Gere having just played Hamlet.) At this point, it's important to sniff the cork of the bottle being decanted. Then attach the sniffed cork to the neck of the decanter – the rough equivalent of returning to the patient an organ that's just been surgically removed.

Cellar and Storage

Bluffers shouldn't be afraid to talk about their wine cellar – even if they don't have anything remotely resembling an underground storeroom. A "cellar," for the bluffer's purpose, is a term describing a collection of at least two bottles of wine – or even a single bottle, if it's of reasonable quality. (How many penthouses have old-fashioned "cellars"?) Cellars are for storage; that's all you need to know. But if you're keeping wine for any length of time, there are two important rules that you must observe:

(1) In order to keep the corks from drying out and letting air in, keep your bottles *on their side*, or better still, *upside down*. This will look impressively exotic to the uninitiated, but it's actu-

ally the correct way for bottles to lie in boxes when being transported or stored in warehouses.

(2) Keep your wine at a reasonably constant temperature, preferably *not above* 60 degrees Fahrenheit. If you can't manage that, remember that holding a constant temperature of 70 degrees is better than fluctuating between 40 and 60 degrees. Certain Bordeaux vintages which take 10 or 15 years to mature might be greatly improved if they're stored in a centrally heated house or apartment, instead of in a poorly controlled wine cellar. Consider this: why not drink your wine before it has a chance to spoil?

Temperature Control

Serving wine at the so-called right temperature can lead some folks to extreme measures, like baking Bordeaux in a slow oven or putting ice cubes in Sauternes. This is inadvisable, even though wine is surprisingly resilient. Let this rule be your guide: most red wines should be served at room temperature (the French term is *chambre*), and most white wines should be lightly chilled (pop them in the fridge for an hour or in the freezer for 20 minutes. Snobs who cast aspersions on the freezer technique are easy to figure; no doubt they forgot to take the wine out once upon a time.

There's an intermediate state between chilled and *chambre,* and it's called "cellar temperature." Lucky you. This is a very useful term because it can mean the temperature of the wine when you've forgotten to chill it or warm it. In fact, some light red wines, like Beaujolais, are best consumed at this temperature. If a red wine seems too cold, you can suggest that your guests warm it by cupping their hands around their glasses. Use the French term *chaleur de la main,* and you'll see instant reverence in everyone's eyes.

HISTORY

The history of wine is very long and very involved, stretching back long before Roman times. Happily, you have to deal with only the last hundred years because the wines all over Europe and Africa (and almost everywhere else) were wiped out by a plague of lice. This affliction, *Phylloxera vitifoliae,* attacked and destroyed the roots of the vines. Fortunately for us, it took nearly 30 years to do so. During that time, wine growers from Europe and Africa (and almost everywhere else) had a chance to import wild vine roots from California and graft what remained of the really famous grape varieties onto them. Chalk one up for Uncle Sam.

TASTING, TALKING, DRINKING, AND SERVING

Bluffers should never forget that tasting and drinking wine are two distinctly different kettles of fish and should never be confused. (WARNING: Any wine that tastes like a kettle of fish should not be drunk.) Tasting is an *un*pleasant professional activity which people do for a living. It's done standing up and involves rude noises, contorted faces, and spittoons. (Instructions later.) Tasters *never* swallow. Well, hardly ever. One man in a pinstripe suit at a Muleshoe, Texas, tasting was heard asking another, "What do you think of the Niederhausen Hermannshöhle Spätlese 1982?" The other man paused before replying, "Ah cain't remember, but it shore went down smooth."

Drinking, on the other hand (as opposed to tasting), is pure pleasure. It's done sitting down—except at cocktail parties, which are rarely any fun anyway. If you're sitting down and drinking decent wine, however, you should go through some of the *motions* of tasting, but do so in a wholly different spirit. For one thing, there should be no spitting in mixed company.

The motions of tasting are

(1) Pour about a quarter of a glass. Stare at it. Look discerning. If it's red, tilt the glass and hold it against a white surface. Yours isn't to question why.

(2) Hold the glass firmly by the base and swirl it either clockwise or counterclockwise, but not both at the same time. Swirling requires a little practice. Swirl too hard and you'll spill the wine; swirl too little and you'll get no effect. Supposedly all this swirling releases the bouquet. Actually, you're just showing off.

(3) Having swirled, sniff. An impressively needle-shaped nose helps. Blocked sinuses don't. Some people favor moving the nose from side to side over the wine, presumably to give each nostril its share, but this can look sinister. Restrain yourself.

(4) Only after these preliminaries is it okay to take the liquid into your mouth. A large sip is required, but not too large a sip. Now you've got to perform the most difficult trick of all — taking in a small amount of air with an audible sucking noise at the same time as the wine enters your mouth. This is supposed to aerate the wine in your mouth and release more flavor. It's *not* the same as gargling. Don't ever gargle wine — unless you have a sore throat.

(5) **Guardedly Optional.** Having swirled the wine around in your mouth, spit the wine out as elegantly as possible into a spittoon/box of sawdust/potted plant/purse. There's a set spitting order at some tastings. Watch out for this or you might get Bordeaux in your ear as you lean forward to spit. Of course, it's okay to spit Bordeaux in your own ear, if you can — and want to.

To sum up, when drinking a good wine, or one your host considers good, limit yourself to tilting, swirling, and sniffing. Do these things with a gracious smile,

rather than with the fixed, suspicious stare of the professional taster (or one who fears he's being poisoned). Unless you're proficient, don't try to suck in air with the wine. You won't be invited again, for one thing. For another, someone may try to administer the Heimlich maneuver on you.

If you're the host, you'll want to treat as sacrosanct the serving traditions you like and cavalierly dismiss those you hate or find stuffily affected.

These are the most fun:

- Opening the bottle at the dinner table. It lets you show off your virtuoso cork-popping performance, and it'll get you gratifying ooohs and aaahs.
- Using the correctly shaped glass for the wine you're serving – either the tulip-shaped, all-purpose glass if you're trying for a democratic, less-is-more image or a shelf filled with the whole gamut of specialized stemware (sherry, port, flute, etc.) if you're after the more-is-more look.

Of the truckload of traditions that are just too pretentious, here's some you'll probably want to trash (with much verbal derision):

- Wrapping a napkin around the bottle while pouring (to say nothing about worrying about *which direction* you wrap it). Napkins serve only to hide the label. Of course, if you've got a label that needs to be hidden (Thunderbird or Mogen David), you'll have to hang onto this wrapping technique.
- Using one of those little wicker serving baskets that everyone has from the ubiquitous Pier 1 store.
- Letting the wine breathe. You'll probably end up making it dishwater warm.

Seriously, though, people *are* serious about wine—so serious, in fact, that many people feel that drinking (or tasting or serving) wine isn't enough. They're driven to *talk* about it. Some social gatherings seem to revolve around nothing but talking about wine. If you find this boring, you're not alone. But as a bluffer, you'll need to be able to drink and taste wine properly, and you'll have to hold up your conversational end in wine-speak.

Granted that wine-speak is a complicated subject, all you really need to know are a few simple rules.

(1) Don't use wine words except when absolutely necessary. Noises—either a noncommittal "Hmmm . . . ?" or an enthusiastic "Mmmm . . . Aaah!"—and facial contortions—like raised eyebrows, narrowed glances, and pursed lips—are often adequate and don't commit you to anything. Your fraudulent facade is safe.

(2) The word "Yes" is quite sufficient for most taste tests. "Yes" can be said in an infinite variety of tones—doubtfully, quizzically, interrogatively, tentatively, affirmatively, decisively, appreciatively, enthusiastically, or ecstatically. It can be repeated, and it can also be uttered in a clipped, conversation-stopping manner: "Yes! Yes!" or in an excited, rising tone, "Yesyesyes!"

(3) Stall for time. Delay as long as possible describing what the wine actually tastes like. Then limit yourself to some of the following "technical" expressions.

(a) Mention *ullage. Ullage* is the level of wine in the bottle. If you've noticed that the bottle isn't completely full, say in a knowing voice,

"Ah, slightly *ullaged.*" It well could be that your host has swigged some of it beforehand.

(b) Ask whether the wine has "settled." Settling, of course, refers to the guck at the bottom of the bottle (not to the kind of wine you can afford as opposed to the kind of wine you wish you could afford—hence you "settle" for the former).

(c) If it's a red wine, and you've noticed when tilting it that it leaves a thick, transparent tail on the glass (most red wines do), say that it has "good legs."

Appearance

When you've exhausted these strategies, start to talk about the wine's color. You're on fairly safe ground here—unless you're color blind. A person who's just given up golf because he can't distinguish the ball from the grass just might startle fellow guests if he comments about the beautiful, deep *green* Bordeaux. Most people are much better at describing visual phenomena than being precise about tastes or smells. It also might be a good idea to study your metals and semi-precious stones. Describe a wine's colors in terms of gold, amber, garnet, or ruby.

Smell

It's okay to talk about smell, but don't *use* the word "smell." This word always has unpleasant connotations. Nose (in wine lingo, this word *doesn't* have unpleasant connotations), aroma, or bouquet are in-words, correct terminology.

If a certain wine doesn't smell like anything at all, don't comment. Blow your nose; you might have a cold. If the wine still doesn't smell like anything, say acidly, "Pretty *neutral* bouquet."

On the other hand, if it smells *very* strong, say, "Very *intense* bouquet." None of these comments, of course, commits you to an opinion about the wine's quality, but if you feel that you have to be more specific, here's some of the more commonly used "nose" words:

- **oaky, buttery, vanilla-ey** – all used interchangeably to describe certain wines which spend a long time in oak barrels, especially some California Chardonnays and Cabernets.
- **black curranty** – used only when you've made sure that the wine is made from the Cabernet Sauvignon grape.
- **spicy** – ditto, substituting Gewürztraminer for Cabernet Sauvignon. "Spicy" is a vague term, considering how many different spices there are, but these things don't worry the connoisseur – or the bluffer.
- **yeasty** – a fashionable term to use when talking about champagne. Don't try to figure it out.

The fact is, though, that wines can smell like *anything* – violets, truffles, beets, sweaty saddles, wet socks, farmyards, or gasoline (old Rieslings often have a curious, oily smell). Smells are oddly evocative, but most descriptions are entirely personal. There's nothing to stop you from trying this tactic – the more personal the better – because it can't be disproved. Remark, for instance, "This wine reminds me of a week I spent in

New Jersey. I don't know exactly what the connection is—the wild flowers, the sea air, the New York City smog off in the distance ..."

Taste

Wines can taste sweet or dry (not sweet) or acid. It's that simple—too simple, in fact. However, no one has come up with any other precise words to describe the various tastes of wine. All the rest are metaphors—a poet's dream and a bluffer's nightmare. But don't give up. You can get a lot of miles out of those three key adjectives.

Sweet and Dry

Degrees of sweetness and dryness are obvious, but in wine-speak, there's no shame in stating the obvious. It's especially impressive if you know how sweet or how dry a wine is *supposed* to be, and then suggest that this particular wine somehow "contradicts expectations." Therefore, you might well comment, "Sur*pris*ingly dry for a Beerenauslese" or "This Chablis isn't as *bone* dry as I would have expected." Both of these opinions are effective because they show that (a) you know your stuff and (b) you have original opinions (even if they're wrong).

Almost all red wines are dry, so there's not much point in saying that a Bordeaux is "surprisingly dry." And, remember, if you insist on being original and say that your host's Chianti is "surprisingly sweet," you may not get a second glass. Know your reds.

Acid

Talking about acidity will make you sound instantly knowledgeable. Acidity in wine is a good thing (believe it or not), so a noncommittal "good acidity" can work wonders. This is especially true of white wines, where acidity implies freshness. A white wine with too little acidity can be criticized for being heavy, flat, or simply "fat." (see Body)

Wines, of course, can be *too* acid. This is sometimes a fault of wines that come from cold countries and certain frigid regions in Germany and New York. Comments on excess acidity are often expressed with furrowed facial contortions.

Wine contains different kinds of acidity. The best kinds, tartaric and lactic, for instance, don't have an overwhelming taste; instead, they impart freshness ("zinginess," or some other word beginning with a "z," if you prefer). Other kinds of acidity which you can clearly taste include malic acid, which makes wine taste like apples (not necessarily a bad thing); "appley" is an apt description for Mosel wines, for instance. The *worst* kind of acidity is acetic, which makes the wine taste like vinegar. If you think a wine tastes "vinegary," and you don't want to upset your host, observe that the wine is "*très* acidic, *nicht wahr?*" You've aced the evening.

Balance

Even "good acidity" isn't enough, though. A wine needs to be *balanced.* Balance is perhaps *the* key concept in the wine world. Fortunately, nobody ever asks exactly what's balanced with what. Everyone, though, knows that the constituent parts of wine—alcohol, acidity, and sweetness – should be roughly in harmony. Unbalanced wines are boringly predictable; they're usually very dull and very, very ordinary. Like a perfectly balanced person, a perfectly balanced wine is dazzling, a rare and wondrous miracle.

Tannin

Here's a user-friendly term for the wine bluffer: tannin is a preservative extracted from the grape skins and seeds and is found mainly in red wines. It's easily recognizable because it grips the back of your teeth like those little spit suckers that the dentist inserts in your mouth. Young red wines are especially likely to be tannic. Remember that "hard" and "tannic" are two adjectives that go together. You'll know precisely what we mean if you ever taste young Bordeaux – one of the most *un*pleasant of all experiences. Thus, if you're given a Bordeaux and discover that it's about as pleasant and yielding as an IRS agent, you should say, "Still pretty tannic." But there's a danger here. Some wines – like some tax auditors – go from being unpleasantly hard and tannic (too young) to being unpleasantly dried out (too old) without the middle ground of pleasant mellowness.

Fruit

This might seem the most obvious quality of a wine's taste. After all, fruit is the starting point of wine, the substance it's made from. So to say that a wine is "fruity" is to suggest that it has gone through all the processes which have transformed it from uninteresting grapes into a miraculous drink – all for nothing.

"Fruity" should be the bluffer's last resort. "Grapey" is a different matter because only wines made from certain kinds of grapes, especially Muscat, *should* taste like grapes.

Body

This is essential. Unlike certain chic, well-heeled women, wines generally aspire to be full-bodied. Wines with insufficient body are "thin," which *isn't* a compliment. On the other hand, wines with too much body are called "fat," which likewise is not complimentary. Male wine enthusiasts, especially the Europeans, often talk about wine in female terms—for example, "This (pointing to a bottle of wine) is the beautiful girl you take to the opera . . . but *this* (beaming and caressing another bottle) is the woman you marry." This type of analogy could well account for the reason some European chauvinistic men seem to enjoy wine more than women.

Other Descriptions

There are other approaches to talking about the taste of wine, including the ambiguous, all-embracing term "pronounced." "This wine has a *pronounced* bouquet, don't you think?" is safe and more or less meaningless, which is, after all, what you're aiming for.

Great Vintages of the Past

Vintages are like eighteenth-century battles. The French win most of them, the Germans and the Americans have an occasional, brilliant victory, and the Italians don't even try.

It's impressive, though completely useless, to reel off a few of the great years of the past. Try 1870 (that particular Bordeaux took 80 years to age, which must have been disastrous for the original purchasers) and another great pair of years—1899 and 1900. Good vintages, in fact, often come in pairs; there's 1928 and 1929, 1961 and 1962, 1970 and 1971, and 1982 and 1983. (There's been some happy talk about the superb French harvest in 1989, so you might profitably take a look at 1990 too—just in case.) On the other hand, good vintages also come singly: 1945, 1959, 1966, and in trios: 1947, 1948, 1949. Come to think of it, good vintages come whenever they darn well please.

Several things to note here are

(1) when talking about great vintages, people always seem to mean great Bordeaux vintages.
(2) great Bordeaux vintages occur (on the average) two out of every three years.
(3) "vintages of the century" occur at least twice a decade.

If someone says, "1928 was a *wonderful* vintage for Bordeaux," the bluffer can retort, "Yes, but very poor for Tokay," or "Yes, but a freak rainstorm practically destroyed the vintage in the Barossa valley." It's highly unlikely that the other person will know anything about old vintages in obscure areas. You might also opine that Des Moines, Iowa, has never had a good year for Bordeaux.

BUYING WINE

Buying wine on impulse, like choosing a Vice President on impulse, can be a *grave* mistake. Decide first whether you want the wine for

(1) immediate consumption
(2) aging
(3) drinking in large quantity (fraternity parties, weddings, etc.)
(4) drinking in small quantity and/or quality drinking (dinner parties, splitting a bottle with your current squeeze, etc.)

Then decide what price you can afford for your purpose and stick to it.

There are lots of places to buy wine, and this plethora of possibilities poses a problem for the pluffer — er, bluffer: where to buy wine — and admit to buying it there. Basically, you've got three options.

The Biggies

There are two kinds: the football-size grocery-liquor-drug one-stops and the huge liquor-only types. These places have forced themselves into first place by their sheer size and muscle power. There are obvious advantages to buying wine there. At the one-stop, you can buy toilet paper, lettuce, and Château Marmoset all at the same place. These giants are so big that they can sell a lot of things cheaply, but they're also very good at convincing you that they're cheaper than anywhere else in town, and this isn't necessarily true. However, they usually do have a decent variety of wines.

The biggies, however, also have disadvantages:

(1) They're often horrible places, filled with screaming toddlers and gum-chewing teeny-boppers at the checkout.
(2) They're *too* big, and, therefore, they buy wine in enormous lots, which rules out many interesting, little-known regional wines.
(3) If you do find a wine you like in a supermarket and serve it to your friends, there's a good chance that they will know exactly where it comes from and exactly how much it costs. "This Château Bon Marché of yours is terrific! $4.95 from Piggly Wiggly, isn't it?"

Specialty Wine Shops

These places have some advantages over supermarkets. First, they're smaller, so they can both buy and sell wine on a more personal basis. They're usually friendlier, and sometimes they even have people working in them who know something about wine.

However, be careful of the specialty stores that cater to the snooty wannabees or to the upper class themselves. Usually, their salespeople have all been to private prep schools and colleges and wear Rolex (usually counterfeit) watches. They tend to expect similar standards from their customers. You won't feel at home in one of these places unless you're an investment banker (or Zsa Zsa Gabor).

Ed's Liquor Store & Tattoo Parlor

These small, seedy here-today, gone-tomorrow joints inevitably come at the bottom of the list. They're the source of those poisonous bottles of Thunderbird and Mad Dog 20/20 that give you incredible hangovers after BYOB parties. In addition, their prices are often ridiculous, and it's unusual to see bottles properly stored there. The people who run these kinds of stores tend to own pit bulls that lie in wait and growl at you as you enter. And they never cash two-party checks. However, they do have one advantage: they're open when you need them most—late at night.

Wines at Auction

People romanticize auctions. They love the eagle-eyed auctioneer with his hammer, bow tie, and superhumanly quick patter, all the cryptic gestures, the icy fear of involuntarily raising an eyebrow and inadvertently buying an old master, and the eternal hope of discovering a fantastic bargain. Practically speaking, though, in the case of wine auctions, most of these romantic fantasies should be corked. A lot of wine finds its way to the auction rooms as a last resort—because it's gone bad. Bargains *are* possible, but auctions are a high-risk venture, and the buyer is strongly advised to taste the wine first.

There's one additional way to obtain wine which meets the requirement of being inexpensive and impressive to your friends. There are companies which produce "look alike" labels of famous and not-so-famous vintages. Simply find a wine you like at your local supermarket, remove the original label, and slap on one of your dummy labels. Your guests will drive themselves nuts trying to figure out how you could afford to serve them a Château Lafite-Rothschild 1956, when in reality the label really says (in ultrafine print) that it was produced by the same vineyard that publishes MAD magazine. Think of the joy you'll have imagining your friends' conversation on the drive home from your party.

Understanding the Label

The neophyte wine bluffer has yet another problem to tackle: decoding labels. This can often be confusing, and the worst offenders of this cryptic double-talk are probably the Germans, who compound the sin of overcomplicating their wine nomenclature by using unreadable, barbed-wire Gothic lettering. If you can understand a German wine label, you can fathom anything. For example:

A German imperial eagle	Fascist tendencies?
NAHE	it comes from the Nahe region
1976er	easy, the vintage
Niederhausen	it comes from a small town called Niederhausen

Hermannmunster	it comes from a vineyard called Hermannmunster in the town of the same name (not from the tall guy with bolts in his neck)
Riesling	it's made from Riesling grapes
Auslese	it's made from selected, late-gathered grapes
Qualitätswein mit Prädikat	it's a quality wine, and it has a title
Amtliche Prufüngsnummer (A.P. Nr.) 1 750 053/51/77	totally irrelevant
Verwaltung der Staatliche Weinbaudomänen Niederhausen-Schlossböckelheim	the most important information of all, the grower
e	mysterious letter, something to do with the EEC
0.7l	contains only 700 ml (70 cl) — not 750, the bastard

If German wine labels contain too much information (and they usually do), others often contain too little. Wines from Greece and Cyprus are prime examples. They're always named after the ancient gods (Aphrodite, Bacchus), tragic heroes (Othello, Orestes), or bathroom cleaners (Demestica). Their labels tell you nothing about the vintage, region, or anything else you might want to know. Given the quality of most Greek wines, this probably is a very sensible policy.

In general, concerning labels, look for

(1) The vintage. This is usually clearly visible. Some wines don't have vintages, and they're known as non-vintage (say "NV"). The only acceptable non-vintage wines are champagne and sherry.

(2) The grape variety. Don't expect to see this in all cases. Very stately wines (Bordeaux and Burgundy, for example) don't specify their grape variety; you're expected to know it.

(3) The country of origin. *Always* look for this. Some German-looking bottles carry the international mark of shame –"EEC Tafelwein." This means that the wine has been dredged up from the EEC wine lake and bottled by bureaucrats.

(4) The region. Look for letters like AC, DOC, etc. These cryptic abbreviations mean only that the wines come from a designated area. With French wines, this is good. With Italian wines, this is generally bad.

(5) Bottling information. This shows whether the wine has been bottled at a château or estate (always considered a good thing) and the city of origin (Detroit- or Cleveland-bottled wines are to be avoided).

Authorities on Wine

Everyone likes to feel they can rely on their favorite authority on a subject (although the purpose of this bluffer's guide is to make every reader his or her own authority). Likewise, the wine bluffer should have some opinions about the leading wine buffs.

Hugh Johnson is in a class all his own. It's become almost mandatory for any wine publication which is going to succeed to have a Hugh Johnson reference. There isn't only an ever-growing list of Hugh Johnson wine books (not all of them exclusively written by the great man), but there's also a wide range of Hugh Johnson wine accessories. There's even a rumor that Hugh himself may soon be available as a wine accessory. **Tasting note:** elegant, well-balanced, high-class Bordeaux of impeccable style, but very high recent output may be prejudicing quality.

Michael Broadbent is the next best thing. Broadbent combines writing his interesting and authoritative wine books with rushing around the world as an international wine personality. **Tasting note:** racy, elegant appearance; mature but aging well. Slightly volatile.

Robert Parker is a superb wine guru. He's achieved this excellence by awarding various "grades" to various wines (reminds us of school days when we were given grades out of a possible 100); most wines are never less than 60/100. **Tasting note:** 86/100 is usually very sound, occasionally a little too assertive.

WINES AROUND
THE WORLD

There are more than 4,000 named varieties of the domesticated grape. Don't panic. Some wiseacres claim to be able to distinguish more than 30 by taste, but for practical purposes, you can get by with less than a dozen.

The top ten grape varieties are:

(1) Cabernet Sauvignon (cab-er-*nay* saw-veon-*yohn*) Probably France's most famous red Bordeaux grape; now also grown in California, Australia, Spain, Italy, Bulgaria, etc. It's become the world's number-one red grape, perhaps because of its bold, spicy taste. It tastes roughly the same wherever the grapes are grown, which is extremely practical: you always know what you'll be getting.

(2) Chardonnay (shar-doe-*nay*) *The* most famous French grape used to make white Burgundy. It's also grown in California, Australia, Spain, Italy, Bulgaria, etc. As the world's number one white grape, it too tends to taste roughly the same wherever it's grown.

(3) Chenin Blanc (shay-nan-*blahn*) The best-known white grape in the Loire Valley (and also in California). Surprisingly, it's the most revolting grape variety in the world because it often produces wines which smell and taste like vomit.

In favored corners of the Loire, however, it somehow manages to produce some of the best dry and sweet wines in the world. But in less favored corners, it produces a lot of very ordinary sparkling wine.

(4) Gewürztraminer (gay-*vertz*-traw-me-ner) Grown in Germany and in Germanic sections of France (Alsace) and Italy (Alto Adige). Also known as Traminer, but that tag was apparently too short and too easy to pronouce. This particular grape imparts a very pronounced, pungent, spicy aroma and rich flavor. You tend to either love it or hate it.

(5) Merlot (mer-*low*) The other red Bordeaux grape (also grown in California, Italy, Bulgaria, etc.). It often makes more palatable wines than Cabernet Sauvignon, but it's less tough and less tannic. According to authorities, it isn't supposed to be as good, presumably because wines made from it don't taste as bold.

(6) Pinot Noir (pee-no-no-*whar*) A red grape of notoriously difficult, temperamental character — kind of like Solzhenitsyn, Ovid, and the Chicago Black Sox. It goes into a decline when exiled — in this case, from its native lands of Burgundy and Champagne.

(7) Riesling (*reez*-ling) The most important thing about this grape is to pronounce its name correctly. Say "Reez-ling," not "Rice-ling." The next most important thing about it is that a lot of so-called Rieslings (for example, Wälschriesling, grown in Hungary, and the Yugoslav Rajnski Rizling) are not real Rieslings at all, but part of

an Eastern European ampelographic con. The *true* Riesling is Germany's finest grape; it makes rather tart wines, which you're supposed to call "steely." When they get older, you call them "oily." There's a little-known variant called Diesling, which is used to fuel semis.

(8) Sauvignon Blanc (saw-veen-*yohn*-blahn) A fashionable white grape variety, fairly tart; it's supposed to impart the smell of crushed nettles. This is the grape used to make Sancerre and Pouilly-Fumé, which is why in California (where they grow it, like everything else), it's called Fumé Blanc.

(9) Sémillon (*say*-me-yohn) Possibly the world's most unappreciated white grape. Unfortunately, it's highly susceptible to rot. Nonetheless, the Australians have planted a lot of them, and they seem to thrive down there.

(10) Syrah (sear-*rah*) Possibly the world's most unappreciated red grape; it's used to make the great northern Rhône wines. The Aussies like this one as well, but call it Shiraz, which sounds classier in Australia.

Other good grape varieties to know are Gamay, a purple grape used to make Beaujolais, but strangely not much else, and Muscadet, a grape variety which gives its name to a light, dry white wine and doesn't taste like much of anything; don't confuse it with Muscat, a grape which imparts a *very* strong taste of the Muscat grape itself. For some really obscure varieties, try the French Viognier (used only to make Condrieu and Château-Grillet). Also the Catalan Xarel-lo, with its uniquely hyphenated double "l," and the German Ortega, which is named after the Spanish philosopher Ortega y Gasset, reportedly one of the great closet winos of his time.

France

Overrated. The bluffer can get considerable mileage by saying that France has been resting on its laurels for far too long, that its wines are overpriced, and that better value can be obtained elsewhere. However, this ploy needs to be backed up by at least a skeletal knowledge of the major French wine areas because no matter how much you criticize France, it remains the number-one wine country. French wines are the ones that everyone else tries to imitate.

The Châteaux of Bordeaux

Wines from Bordeaux are the most snobbish of all wines. The châteaux were classified in 1855 according to 1st, 2nd, 3rd, 4th, and 5th growths, and you should at least know the names of the first growths: Château Lafite-Rothschild, Château Latour, Château Margaux, Château Haut-Brion (try calling it O'Brien, which may be the derivation), and Château Mouton-Rothschild.

A few other châteaux worth mentioning are Pétrus (the most expensive of all), Cheval Blanc (from the village of St. Emilion, a good one for the bluffer to praise), Palmer (comment on its powerful, yet delicate taste) and La Mission-Haut-Brion (be sure to say that it's *far* better than Laville-Haut-Brion.)

Naturally, all of these wines are too expensive to drink, so let people know that you know that they've become a commodity rather than a drink, that Bordeaux itself has become a stock market, and that it's probably eading for a crash. The only trouble is that people have already been saying this for a long time, and the last crash occurred in 1974.

As far as actually drinking Bordeaux, the bluffer (unless extremely rich) has two options: one is to avoid it altogether on the grounds that the prices are inflated because of speculators; the other is to find a little-known château, either an obscure *cru bourgeois* (a wonderful category below the *cru classé,* the classified growths), or a château from an obscure area like Bourg, Blaye, or Fronsac. This may or may not be top-drawer wine, but it'll certainly be good bluffing material because very few other people will have heard of those châteaux.

Burgundy

Burgundy is the number-one longtime rival of Bordeaux, and you're not bluffing when you swear on your sainted mother's life that the best white Burgundies are *the* most sought-after dry whites in the world. All snooty connoisseurs express a deep fondness for red Bordeaux and white Burgundy, so you should go a step further and praise any white Burgundy called Meursault, Corton-Charlemagne, or anything to do with Montrachet; these Burgundies are all very special experiences. Burgundy is the best thing to order with a fish course – as long as somebody else gets stuck with the check.

Red Burgundy is secretly the favorite drink of many of the above connoisseurs, but it's been in a slump lately. Some people say the "new style" (don't worry about what this means; nobody really knows) is thin and weak. Others say that the "old style" was mainly Algerian. One wine merchant who specializes in the stuff recently declared that 90 percent of it is "junk."

The Burgundy bluffer must get his priorities right if he wants to seem to be a four-star professional. The crucial factor in Burgundy is the grower—not the village or the vineyard or the vintage. A village like Aloxe-Corton, for instance, contains about 40 vineyards, divided up (because of peculiar inheritance laws) among hundreds of different growers, and only a handful of them are any good.

Some growers' and shippers' (*négociants*) names to bandy about are

Domaine de la Romanée-Conti He owns some of the most famous of all of the Burgundy vineyards—for example, Romanée-Conti, La Tâche, and part of Chassagne-Montrachet. No one can afford these wines, so it's safe to say that they're overrated and overpriced.

Louis Latour He's a grower—and controversial. It's best to say that his whites are infinitely better than his reds. The latter, some whisper, are pasteurized.

Armand Rousseau He makes great Chambertin. This wine is superb when it's at its very best, but some vintages have a tendency to get cloudy and fizzy. Sorry, "sparkling."

Daniel Rion He's "new style," a technical and trendy grower who has very good Nuits-St.-Georges, even in bad years. Rion is a very good bluffer's ace-in-the-hole because he's not yet particularly well known, but, unfortunately, he's just as expensive as anybody who is.

Alsace

"Alsatian is ze dog," the great wine writer André

Simon once remarked, and many German shepherds and wine growers would agree.

Alsace has great difficulty deciding whether it's French or German. At present, it's decided to be French, but this is hard to believe when they still speak German and eat sauerkraut. The wines from Alsace reflect this national schizophrenia. They taste half-German (grapey) and half-French (dry). Some people find this unacceptable and think Alsace growers should make up their minds once and for all.

The rudest thing you can safely say about Alsatian wines is that they're an "acquired taste." Rude or not, this remark should not be taken lightly because it's true, and the bluffer should try to *acquire* a taste for Alsatian wines because they are loved by the world's topnotch wine gurus (and besides, Alsace is a little-known area, a bluffing nugget for the aggressive bluffer.)

You'd do well to also remember that Alsatian wines are all named after grape varieties—that is, Riesling, Gewürztraminer, etc. It's becoming fashionable to criticize the latter by saying something like "Too obvious. Even an ignoramus can detect it in blind tastings." Then turn around and praise the Tokay-Pinot-Gris with a "Now *that's* more subtle." Another good variety to mention is a "yuppie" variety: Pinot Blanc. Conversely, Alsace's Sylvaner attracts whatever the opposite of "yuppie" is.

For a relatively obscure Alsatian wine, mention Auxerrois, but sigh deeply and lament that its one-time dark intensity has been compromised.

Growers and shippers are the next most important things to remember about Alsace. There are an infinite number of them, but you have to know only a couple. Johnny Hugel is definitely a name to drop. He's kind of an ambassador of Alsatian wines and wears a baseball cap. Whatever you say about his wines, you *must* stress that they're very different from those of Hubert Trimbach. Trimbach is a younger version of Johnny Hugel, without the cap. His wines are *totally* different.

We can't stress enough the bluffing potential that Alsace holds. The vineyards there are all the rage now. They were always there, of course, but the Alsatians didn't want to confuse people by mentioning them. Now, however, they've decided that people need to be confused a little and have introduced a category of Alsace *grand cru* for twenty-five vineyards. (You don't need to know any of them.)

Alsatian wines are mostly very dry with the exception of the special late-gathered and noble-rot-affected ones called Vendange Tardive and Selection de Grains Nobles. There are the equivalent (well, almost) of the German Auslese and Beerenauslese. But don't mention this similarity when you're with Germans and/or Alsatians because they don't seem to like each other very much. Strange, since neither have NFL football teams.

Vintages are quite important in Alsace. 1983 and 1985 were both very good. For the sweet wines, 1976 is the classic vintage, and it might be a good idea to praise lesser-known vintages like 1979 and 1981.

Champagne

Good champagne is vastly expensive, and in order to sell it, the French have managed to convince the world that it's essential to posh, luxurious living; seemingly, there's nothing quite like it. There's some truth to that. Of all the classic French wines, champagne seems to be the most difficult to imitate. It's still the only sparkling wine that has more than a 50 percent chance of being palatable.

Champagne is both an area and a method. It's grown in a bitterly cold region east of Paris, too far north for any sensible grape to ripen. In fact, a lot of champagne grapes don't *ever* ripen, which is why you get indigestion after wedding receptions (unless you're the father of the bride and have other reasons for having indigestion). Champagne comes in varying degrees of dryness, and they are, in decreasing order: Brut, Extra Dry, Dry, Demi-Sec, Doux, and Riche. But you'll probably never see any Doux or Riche unless you're in Russia, where they prefer their champagnes very sweet.

The thing for the bluffer to be most aware of with champagne is that it's made by a fiendishly complicated process. This involves a tangle of intricate steps — for example, twisting and angling the bottles (*rémuage*), adding small amounts of sugar and brandy (*dosage*), and leaving it in a cellar for a couple of years (*âge*). Fortunately, the process is *so* complicated that very few people can explain it convincingly. You'll bluff best by calling the process by its French name, *méthode champenoise.*

One of the more unlikely stories about champagne is that it was invented by a monk called Dom Pérignon. Not so. Dom Pérignon is the name of the most expensive champagne of Moët & Chandon, the biggest (but by no means the best) of the champagne houses.

The best champagne firm is supposed to be Krug. They certainly get away with selling their non-vintage champagne for twice as much as anyone else. Other names to be familiar with are Bollinger and anyone who has anything in common with Perrier (except the water) – Joseph Perrier, Perrier-Jouët, and Laurent Perrier all make good bubbly.

Most champagne is non-vintage (don't forget: say "NV"). It's often said that non-vintage is the *true* champagne, and that vintage and the deluxe brands in fancy bottles have more to do with marketing than with quality. This sounds like sour grapes – and probably is.

The Loire

In the Loire Valley, there's a good argument for sticking to the châteaux and forgetting the other wines; the latter are noted for their unrelentingly high acidity, and they're frequently made from the disgusting Chenin Blanc grape. Two fashionable exceptions are Muscadet and Sancerre. One of the best-kept secrets is that Muscadet doesn't taste like much of anything. It's extremely hard to identify in blind tastings. Sancerre and its neighbor, Pouilly-Fumé, on the other hand, are the easiest of all wines to identify in blind tastings. It's a good idea for the bluffer to knock these fashionable names. Anyway, they're not the best Loire wines. The best are the dry Savennières and Vouvray and the sweet Bonnezeaux, pronounced "bonzo" (the same as the name of one of Ronald Reagan's earliest political cronies), and Quarts de Chaume (car-duh-showm). The last two are much better than the well-publicized Moulin Touchais, and very few people have heard of them. As a result, they're absurdly cheap.

There's also some very good red wine bluffing potential in the Loire. The best of these is Bourgueil. Don't confuse it with Bourgogne (French for "Burgundy") or

Bourg, a small town near Bordeaux. It's made from the Cabernet Franc grape. The vintage should usually be the latest or the one before that. With the sweet wines, the older the better.

The Rhône

Rhône wines are mainly red. You don't need to worry too much about the whites, which are either very rare or very expensive (Condrieu, Château Grillet) or else not as good as the red equivalent.

The best northern Rhône wine is Hermitage. It's a "manly" wine and was added to Château-Lafite in the last century. Since Hermitage is often too strong to drink on its own and Château-Lafite is often too weak, it made sense to blend the two wines. This alchemy wouldn't be allowed these days, of course.

It's agreed that the best Hermitage grower is Gérard Chave ("Marvelous wine, but an eccentric guy"). Côte Rôtie, which sounds a little like something from a cheap French menu, is the other praiseworthy northern Rhône wine. State that, in your humble opinion, it's better than Hermitage. The grower to mention here is Etienne Guigal. Crozes-Hermitage (crowz-air-me-taj) is a weaker, cheaper form of Hermitage.

The southern Rhône is easy. Here, there's only one really famous wine – the strong red Châteauneuf-du-Pape. This was once questionable stuff, but its reputation today is definitely on the rebound. It comes packaged in embossed bottles which will impress your friends. A good ploy for the bluffer is to mention *white* Châteauneuf-du-Pape, a wine which was almost unheard of until very recently. (It's heavy, almost sweet.) Conversely, with the other well-known southern

Rhône wine, Beaumes-de-Venise, the best thing to do is to feign allegiance to the little-known red, rather than the sickly sweet white variety. With any luck, the non-bluffer will not know that some supermarkets sell the red for five bucks. It's actually very much like a straightforward Côtes-du-Rhône, and *this* isn't a name to be scorned. Your comment should be: "In its class, it's a *far* better value than Beaujolais."

The Rhône also produces Tavel, one of very few rosés about which you can be polite. However, avoid at all costs, *orange*-colored Tavels.

Vintages A convenient, but unfortunately not entirely true, theory is that since the Rhône is so far south, vintages don't matter. Another theory, also not true, is that good vintages in the north aren't good in the south.

Beaujolais and Mâconnais

These regions are a southern extension of Burgundy and produce some fine, attractive red and white wines. It's a pity, therefore, that the wine everybody has heard of from the region is the generally unpleasant Beaujolais *nouveau*. But it's not wholly surprising that Beaujolais *nouveau* is unpleasant since it's specifically bottled (a) to be drunk much too young and (b) to be transported from France in various unsuitable ways (fast cars, helicopters, pipelines, marathon runners, etc.) for publicity purposes. Bluffers should favorably mention only Beaujolais *nouveau* that's at least five years old. The idea that this wine must be consumed by Christmas is garbage. Say so – loudly.

The Beaujolais wines for the bluffer to get enthusiastic about are the little-known wines or *crus*. Fleurie

' provide

rap group

any warni

Campbe
without us
only one
need to re
ton himsel

And nei
than the F
an uncontr

KTVX
ABC affili
comment.
ber" of cal
tent of the

television.

uage was also heard in another 40 cities
d "Donahue" on tape later that day.

tly, his intent was to demonstrate ex-
lisgusting these lyrics are. Great. To do
ks to the rappers' level.

later apologized, but what the heck was
inking?

□ □ □

DUMB
Mr. Donah
sales of th
Wanna Be'

Just wha
publicity.

And whi
thank Ch. 2
afternoon

LEEPS: The folks over at Ch. 2 weren't
h the subject matter of that particular
of "Donahue," but they were glad they
w the day after it tapes.

on to the bleeping done by the "Dona-
ucers, KUTV did its "strongest editing

and Moulin-à-Vent are the most fashionable, mainly because they're relatively pronounceable. Brouilly and Côte de Brouilly, which are often just as good, aren't easy to pronounce – or remember.

Mâcon wines are the nearest equivalents for us non-millionaires to buy if we want some white Burgundy. Pouilly-Fuissé, the most famous of them (has nothing to do with Pouilly-Fumé, by the way) isn't worth mentioning because it's grossly overpriced. Plain Mâcon-Villages is perhaps a little common; it can even be found on Chinese restaurant wine lists (generally, the kiss of death). The good bluffer should also mention some of the individual village names, some of which are memorably unusual – for example, Mâcon-Lugny (ma-sewn-loon-yee) and Mâcon-Viré. Louis Latour makes a good Mâcon-Lugny, while Les Genièvres and Duboeuf have good Mâcon wines too.

Vintages Like Burgundy, only less important, is the general rule. 1985 was hailed as the best Beaujolais vintage for 50 years.

French Country Wines

All the other wines in France can be lumped under this convenient heading – and forgotten. There are too many of them to remember. A better value, in any case, can be had from other countries at this level.

Germany

It may surprise people who think of Germany as a northern industrial country full of people driving Audis down autobahns that it's a country with an old, proud wine tradition. It may surprise these same people that

Germany produces some bland, sugary wines (one step up from fruit juice), but it also produces some of the world's greatest, most individual wines. Germany is constantly developing new methods, new grape varieties, and new clones of existing varieties which produce higher and higher yields–up to five times as great as that of less technically minded Spain. The result? Millions and millions of gallons of Liebfraumilch, which all taste the same. But there's another side to the German wine industry, one in which technical skill is put at the service of individuality, sometimes to an almost absurd degree. Up to 20 different wines can be made and marketed from one small patch of vineyard.

As a neophyte bluffer, one of the first things you should know about German wines is that most of them are sweet. And don't do a knee-jerk condemnation of sweet wines. Candy and ice cream are also sweet; why shouldn't some wines be the equivalent of the dessert course rather than the main course? Be aware, however, that the Germans have started to make a lot of their wines dry (*trocken*) and half-dry (*halbtrocken*). These take a little getting used to, but they go well with food. Dry German wines are good bluffing fodder because few people are aware of their existence.

The German system of wine classification is so obsessively logical that it's complete mystifying. Wines are classified, first, according to where they come from. This may sound sensible enough, but it doesn't mean just an area (for example, Mosel-Saar-Ruwer of Rheingau), and often an individual vineyard lies in a tiny village–for example, Niederwallufer Blankenberg. Words ending with *-er* are generally villages; for instance,

Forster, from Forst. But some words ending with *-er* are vineyards; for example, Forster Ungeheuer.

And how about this for logic? There are two wines, one called Zeltingen Sonnenuhr, the other Zeltingen Münzlay. Both come from the village of Zeltingen in the Mosel, right? Right. One comes from the Sonnenuhr vineyard and the other comes from the Müntzlay vineyard, right? Wrong. One comes from the Sonnenuhr, but the other one can come from *any* vineyard in the Zeltingen district.

German quality wines are classified according to the degree of sweetness or ripeness of the grapes from which they're made. Kabinett is riper than the lowest quality grade, QbA (Qualitätswein bestimmter Anbaugebiete), but often not as sweet because QbA *may* be sugared. Spätlese (shpate-lay-zuh) is riper and usually sweeter than Kabinett and so on through Auslese and Beerenauslese up to Trockenbeerenauslese, which may sound dry (*trocken*), but it's *not*. It's very, very sweet because it's made from individually picked grapes shriveled with the noble rot. You'll pay over $150 a bottle for this liquid gold.

There's also Eiswein (ice-vine), which isn't a wine you put in the freezer but one made from grapes picked in late January or February and crushed while still frozen. This is no joke. The wine is rare *and* expensive.

The Germans are known for inventing new grape varieties. However, having invented hundreds of them with peculiar names like Huxelrebe and Optima, they've decided that Riesling is the best, after all. The only really new breed whose name you need to know is Müller-Thurgau because it's the most widely planted grape in Germany. It makes wines which are quick to mature and easy to forget. A couple of good, traditional grape varieties are Sylvaner (makes the best wine in Franconia) and Ruländer. Because they've made their classification system so complicated, the Germans find their quality wines very difficult to sell. However, the beautifully fresh and delicate wines of the Mosel-Saar-Ruwer, the more full-bodied Rheingau, and the sometimes luscious Palatinate wines are often wonderfully cheap.

Growers are crucial in Germany, as they are in Alsace and Burgundy. Some good names to be familiar with are:

J. J. Prüm — A semi-legendary figure who refuses to sell his wine before he considers it ready or to people whom he considers unworthy.

Friedrich Wilhelm Gymnasium — The school that Karl Marx attended in Trier; it has some very good vineyards.

Schloss Vollrads — A famous old castle in the Rheingau, owned by a very tall man with a very long name, Count Matuschka-Greiffenklau.

The Three B's — Bassermann-Jordan, von Bühl, and Bürklin-Wolf, the three biggest estates in the Palatinate region.

Vintages Good, sunny vintages are rare in Germany. 1983, 1976, and some 1971 vintages are the best recent ones. However, wines made in lesser vintages can, after 10, 20, or even 50 years, taste pretty good too.

The Best of the Rest

Italy produces more wine than any other country. It also produces more bad wine than any other country. Some Italian wine is delicious, but very little of it is exported. The Italians, quite understandably, prefer to drink it themselves.

Most of the famous names in Italian wines, like Soave, Valpolicella, and Chianti should be avoided. The best wines tend to be made by mavericks who pay no attention to the rules. The wine bluffer should remember that most people are very sentimental about Italy and allow themselves to believe that just because the towns are beautiful, the wines must also be good. Italian restaurateurs have taken full advantage of the misleading romanticism.

Spain and Portugal are both up-and-coming countries for table wines, wholly unlike both countries' great fortified wines. Rioja has enjoyed immense popularity, partly as a result of its distinctive oaky taste. Some people say this taste is achieved by suspending bags of oak shavings in the wine. Penedès and Ribero del Duero are two Spanish wine regions to watch. In Portugal, try Bairrada (pronounced appropriately, "buy-harder") and the ubiquitous Vinho Verde (vinyo-vaird). Of course, as a consummate bluffer you insist that you drink *only* the more expensive, estate-bottled wines. For a really obscure Portugese wine, try Moscatel de Setúbal, a less trendy substitute for Muscat de Beaumes-de-Venise.

Eastern European wines like the Bulgarian Cabernet-Sauvignon are becoming fashionable these days with the *thirtysomething* crowd. Yugoslavia is on the way up wine-wise too, but the wines of Russia (the third largest producer in the world) have yet to benefit from *perrier-stroika*.

California

Americans have approached winemaking with the same manic enthusiasm which they devote to health, fitness, sex, and football. The results have had the same tendency to be larger than life, but they're now getting better at imitating the subtleties of European wines – the whites, at any rate. The bluffer should claim that you can get better, home-grown Pinot Noir in Oregon than you can in California.

The best California wines are as necessary for you to be acquainted with as the *grand crus* of Bordeaux. However, it's possible to get by with only a fairly small number of reputable names. Of the well-established firms, Robert Mondavi (something of a publicist), Joseph Phelps (admired by the cognoscenti), and Trefethen Vineyards (admirably consistent) are three to mention. Two newer names, which may score some bluffing points are Jordan (for remarkably stylish Cabernet Sauvignon) and Acacia (for Chardonnay which approaches top Chablis in style and quality). Concerning the familiar Paul Masson carafes, the bluffer should critically pronounce the carafes more useful and interesting than the wine inside them.

Australia

It wasn't too long ago that Monty Python was having fun with Perth Pink, Sydney Syrup, and whichever wine it was that had a bouquet like the morning mouth of a duck-billed platypus. Today, wines like Rosemont Chardonnay and Wynns Coonawarra Cabernet Sauvignon are enjoyed by the hoi polloi and the hoity-toity alike. Actually, Australia has probably overtaken California as the wine country that everyone's talking about.

One good reason for this is that the apparently permanent weakness of the Australian dollar makes the wines there an extremely good value. But some of the wines themselves are actually very good, which is almost miraculous, considering that they are produced in a vast dust bowl.

The two key areas to mention are the Hunter and Barossa valleys. It's difficult to remember which is which—and probably unimportant. It's more important to know the names of a few good wineries, such as Brown Bros. in Milawa, Victoria; Penfold's, who makes the legendary Grange Hermitage in south Australia; and Petaluma, which makes about the best Chardonnay outside Puligny-Montrachet.

Possibly Australia's most unique wines are the liqueur Muscats of northeast Victoria. Known as "stickies," these get better the longer they're kept, even though they eventually achieve the color and consistency of pine tar.

New Zealand

No sooner had everyone begun to get excited about New Zealand wines than the government decreed that most of the country's vineyards should be dug up.

Nevertheless, a few New Zealand wines continue to be produced, especially the light and racy whites. A good country for the bluffer to get excited about.

South America

The only important wine countries in South America are Argentina and Chile. Argentina produces an enormous amount of cheap wine. Chile is just the opposite and produces much less wine; however, some of it is of the very highest quality. There are some terrific individual Cabernet Sauvignons (distributed by such fine firms as Miguel Torres and Concha y Toro) and some reasonable Chardonnays. It's even legitimate to get excited about the country's own Gewürztraminer. Chilean Pinot Noir is less successful, and Pinochet is a dictator and shouldn't be mentioned at all.

Two things to note about Chile are: first, the Chilean wine industry goes back to the sixteenth century, and second, Chilean wines were never attacked by the pesky *Phylloxera* louse because, very simply, it is unable to cross the Andes.

WINE IN RESTAURANTS

It's important to remember that restaurants make most of their profits from liquor, and it's not uncommon to find sky-high markups on wine. The situation is even worse in France, where a punitive duty already pushes the price of ordinary wine out of the reach of the *prolétariat*, who need it most. But a markup of 100 percent is considered almost a minimum anywhere, hardly a give-away. Some restaurants get away with charging ridiculous prices because people are willing to fork over $20 for the most basic rotgut in even the least stylish dives. It's depressing to watch. Bear in mind, always, that this wine, often of the most questionable vintage, probably cost the producer about 25 cents to make, and even with shipping and duty and a reasonable profit margin for the grower and merchant, it doesn't cost the restaurant more than four bucks.

The best solution to the problem of wine in restaurants is to bring your own. Unfortunately, some restaurants frown on this practice and charge extravagant corkage fees. Many ethnic restaurants, though, will allow you to bring your own.

If you insist on going to a pretentious, over-rated, four-star restaurant, apart from the near certainty of being ripped off, you're letting yourself in for an elaborate sacrament. Wine stewards are taught to go through a ritual ceremony—handing the wine list to the most important-looking person, pouring out a little for her (or him) to taste, etc. However, the stewards usually don't have a clue about the purpose of these rituals. For this reason, and because most customers are so easily intimidated, wine stewards don't take kindly to having their wines sent back. You may reject a totally dead, flat Mâcon-Villages in a restaurant where the waiter has performed all the right motions with style and panache, only to be told that the wine is *superb* and that it has that very special "typical Mâcon-Village persona."

Here are a few simple rules to follow when ordering wine:

(1) Be polite but firm. Any trace of hesitancy plays right into the hands of the waiter, who invariably will think that you are either stupid, wrong, or just kicking the tires.

(2) If you decide to send the wine back, do it *immediately* after the waiter has given you a small amount to taste. If you delay and start drinking, the waiter will assume that
   (a) you aren't sure
   (b) the wine is drinkable

(3) Claim to be a wine columnist for a prestigious paper or a connoisseur only as a last resort—and only if you're wearing a suit. For some reason, waiters don't believe that people in Levi's ever know anything about wine.

Of course, this kind of heavy-handed tactic shouldn't be necessary. It could ruin a romantic evening. On the other hand, it may be a good pre-matrimonial test. A potential partner who won't allow you to challenge a wine steward may be dictatorial and inelastic in other situations. Conversely, too much wimpy, self-conscious rigidity does not make for a happy honeymoon.

Waiter, This Wine Is Corked — and Other Wine Problems

It's widely believed that in order to qualify as an authenic wine expert, you need to be able to tell whether or not a wine is "corked." So, what's a bluffer to do? Relax. "Corked" is a very ambiguous wine term-let. Some people naively believe that a "corked" wine has cork floating around in it. This isn't the case. Bits of cork, though unsightly, in no way affect the taste of wine. If they did, every bottle would be "corked" because the wine inside is constantly in contact with the cork. Some supercilious and seemingly knowledge-able people say that a corked wine "tastes like cork." Since few of us chew cork for fun, it's easier to ima-gine wine which smells musty and dank, like a house with seepage problems. However, since even experts seem unable to agree on the exact definition of "corked," you might logically conclude that the word is strictly meaningless. Since no one really knows what "corked" means, it's much better to use the term "off." "Off" is anathema to all so-called wine experts.

There are various degrees of "off-ness." Apart from the dank, musty odor, there's oxidation. This is what happens when wine is exposed to the atmosphere. It ends up turning brown and smelling a little burned. With some wines, especially sherry and madeira, this is considered desirable, but the word "madeirized"— that is, tasting like madeira—is a good term of abuse to tuck away and pull out of your back pocket when faced with any wine which is tired or old or has sat around too long. Come to think of it, don't we all know someone who could be characterized as "madeirized"?

Additives and Adulterations

Winemakers committing illegal adulterations have been making news lately. First, there was antifreeze (known to bluffers as ethylene glycol), which makes wine taste fuller and richer and doesn't actually kill anybody, but is poisonous in large doses. But so is wine – in really *large* doses. Therefore the bluffer should always defend antifreeze.

The second was methanol, which is poisonous in very *small* doses. It has killed quite a large number of people. Don't ever defend methanol.

As a result of these scandals, people started to worry about all the other substances which are regularly added to wine. These include cultured yeasts (always used in Australia; perhaps, says one joker, because yeast is the only "cultured" thing down there, mate), sugar beets, sulphur dioxide, tartaric acid, mud, egg whites, pine resin, dried ox blood, and the shredded swim bladder of the sturgeon. Most of these things are not only harmless but actually beneficial. People have tried making organic wine, but it tends to taste like manure. However, many so-called wine coolers also taste like manure to the experts. At this point, you might profitably ask yourself what kind of experts are people who are familiar with the taste of manure?

There are a few treatments of wine which can be justifiably condemned. Filtering through asbestos (a common practice until recently) is probably undesirable, and indeed excessive filtering and centrifuging are now considered a bad thing.

If you find strange little crystals in the bottom of the bottle, remain calm. Smile appreciatively and say, "Ah, *Weinstein!* You don't see it often enough these days. A sure sign that the wine hasn't been abused too much." These crystals are tartaric crystals and are harmless. Other people may not be convinced, but they'll be impressed.

Bluffing with Sherry

Sherry is a fortified wine, like port. However, it's fortified *after* the fermentation has finished, and so it's naturally dry. It's made in a very complicated way, like champagne. You don't need to know how the process works, just the name—the *solera* system.

People who know about sherry generally prefer Fino and Manzanilla, the two driest kinds. These can be delicious, but only if they're fresh. A half-empty bottle, or worse yet, a half-empty decanter, is likely to taste stale and unpleasant. These kinds of sherry should be kept in the fridge and served very cold. Manzanilla, which is actually a Fino that has matured in Sanlucar de Barrameda, always has a salty tang as a result of its proximity to the Atlantic Ocean. Real Amontillado is delicious stuff, but hard to find; like most "medium" products, it's normally too sweet. Genuine Amontillado is supposed to taste nutty.

A lot of bluffing points can be scored by mentioning dry Oloroso, the rarest kind of sherry (and excellent with soup). Sweet Oloroso, better known as Bristol Cream, should be avoided.

Bluffing with Port

Port is an "Englishman's wine." Having lost Bordeaux centuries ago, the British needed another source of wine, and Portugal, a sleepy little country, was happy to accommodate them. Someone with a sweet tooth decided that Douro wine tasted better if its fermentation was stopped half-way though – with sugar still in it. Port has been made that way ever since. There are still a number of English colonials with names like Warre, Graham, and Delaforce running around there as if nothing had happened since the seventeenth century.

Yuppies prefer *vintage* port. This stuff tastes terrible until it's about 20 years old, and, as a result, it's a popular gift to give to babies as a christening present, with the idea that it'll come of age about the same time that the kids do.

Other than vintage, the only thing you should know about port is a little about Tawnies, port that has matured in the barrel rather than in the bottle. This "late-bottled" vintage port isn't really like true vintage at all. For starters, it doesn't have any crud in the bottom. Crusted port, despite not having a vintage, is much more like the real thing (that is, it *does* have crud in the bottom). Any port is particularly suitable if you drink it in a storm.

Bluffing with Madeira

The odd thing about madeira is that it's the only wine that's deliberately boiled. You should know that the process is called the *estufa* system and involves heating the wine to 120 degrees Fahrenheit for a long time. Not surprisingly, it has a distinctively *burned* flavor. The only other thing about madeira to remember is that it has a reputation for its aphrodisiacal qualities. Sales of madeira soared with the release of a novelty song of seduction called "Have Some Madeira, M'Dear."

Bluffing with Brandy

There are a few simple rules to learn about brandy. The first is that the best brandy is made from the worst wine. The second is that brandy is supposed to get better the longer it stays in the barrel but doesn't improve once it's in the bottle. Every year a vast amount of brandy in barrels evaporates away. In Cognac, they call this "the angel's share." If angels can tolerate young brandy, they've got remedies Up There for 3-star hangovers.

It's important to have an opinion on the question of cognac versus Armagnac. Cognac is supposed to be more refined and elegant, Armagnac earthier and more robust. Take your pick, but if you chose cognac, try to avoid the more commercial brands like Martell, Hennessy, and Courvoisier. The connoisseur's brand is Delamain.

An effective anti-snob technique is to have a bottle of very cheap Spanish Fundador or Greek Metaxa 7-Star brandy in reserve. Bring it out with a flourish and pour a snifter for the snob, saying, "I have a kind of *perverse* need for this really *rough* stuff, don't you? It hurts so *good*."

Wine and Food

It's a given that good food and good wine are complementary—the yin and yang of high cuisine. Your simple quiche will be at its best *only* if you serve it with an Alsatian Sauvignon, and your Sauvignon *needs* your quiche to reveal its deepest flavor secrets.

Neither a fine red Burgundy nor a good California Cabernet was created to be swilled by itself, like soda pop. The same is true of the more alcoholic white wines, like white Burgundy or Sauternes. But (and note this "but") *some* lighter wines, mainly white but occasionally red, do a solo act quite nicely. The Bach solo violin partitas of the wine world are the great Rieslings of the Mosel-Saar-Ruwer. The Maximin Grünhaus wines of von Schubert, for instance, are too delicate and fine to share the spotlight with food. The dry Muscats of Alsace are best drunk as an aperitif. The sweeter German Auslese wines aren't really wines to serve with dessert (they don't have enough alcohol); actually, they're desserts in themselves. One sip of Trockenbeerenauslese is probably equivalent to a whole slice of cheesecake. And if you have to have Beaujolais *nouveau*, drink it neat and well chilled.

Oddly enough, however, there are some wines which are traditionally drunk on their own that go as well— if not better—with food. The classic example is sherry. The heavier forms of sherry, Amontillado, and dry Oloroso, are great with all kinds of soups.

As to the problem of *which* wine goes with *what* food, bluffers should never feel intimidated. The golden rule is that there are no golden rules. All rules are made to be broken.

The classic axiom is that only white wines can be served with fish. Admittedly, most fish dishes are best accompanied by white wines—from Muscadet with shellfish to Meursault with, say, sole in a rich cream sauce. But the Basque combination of salt cod and ratatouille is so strong that it needs a red wine to complement it. Some dark-fleshed fish like salmon and fresh tuna go particularly well with a light red. You might try some really outrageous combinations (Châteauneuf with oysters, perhaps, or Coquilles St. Jacques with Zinfandel). The least you can do is to claim to have tried them.

Burgundy is supposed to be the best wine with game, but it all depends on the kind of game. A delicate quail might be overpowered by a heavy Chambertin, for instance, while an equally delicate Margaux might be just the thing. If you're very rich, you're supposed to drink Château d'Yquem with foie gras.

There's also a belief that most cheeses, including the white-rinded ones, like Brie and Camembert, are particularly suited to the finest Bordeaux and Burgundy. This isn't true—even if it does say so in *How to Eat and Drink Like a Yuppie*. White-rinded cheeses completely alter the character of fine red wines, making them taste perversely sweet. Hence, the old wine-trade adage, "Sell on cheese, buy on an apple." But this works only with cheap wines. Château-Lafite-Rothschild with Brie, for instance, is nothing like its true self and might just as well be Beaujolais.

Even cheddar can be too strong and pungent for Bordeaux. The only cheeses that go really well with fine red wine are very hard, subtly flavored ones like the Italian pecorino and the fine Manchego cheeses from Spain. The traditional combination of Ripple and Cheeze-Whiz, on the other hand, can be accorded the bluffer's grudging respect.

GLOSSARY

AC – Neither electricity nor sexual preference, but *Appellation Controllée,* which applies to French wines from designated regions of which certain standards are demanded. This doesn't necessarily mean that they're worth a hoot.

Botrytis Cinerea – Also called the noble rot (which should not be confused in any way with the lineage of British royalty). A fungus essential to producing really sweet, concentrated wines like Sauternes and the German Trockenbeerenauslese.

Bottle-sick – A temporary condition which affects wines immediately after bottling. Not the condition which affects people after drinking too many bottles.

Cap(sule) – A metal or plastic deterrent which covers the cork. Metal ones are fine as long as they're made of lead.

Carmelized – A description of wines which are slightly oxidized.

Cépage – French for "grape variety."

Chaptalization – French for the practice of adding sugar to the "must," or unfermented grape juice; named after Jean Antoine Chaptal, who invented it in the eighteenth century. The French (like breakfast-cereal manufacturers) have shrewdly decided that almost anything sounds better than saying "sugar added."

Château – (a) in France, a castle or stately home; (b) in Bordeaux, any building, outhouse, shed, etc., in which, or near which, wine is made, bottled, or stored.

Château-bottled – Wine which is bottled in the aforementioned building, outhouse, shed, etc.

Commune – French for "parish."

Cru – French for "growth." The best French wines, for some reason, like to call themselves *grand crus* (great growths), *premier crus* (first growths), *premier grands crus*, ad nauseam.

Dégorgement – The ejection of sediment from a bottle.

DOC – Just like AC, only Italian. AC/DOC wines are illegal.

Extract – The aromatic ingredients which make a wine taste good and shouldn't be confused with alcohol, acidity, fruit, or sugar.

Fine – Ethnic term for brandy.

Gouleyant – An excellent French word which means "gulpable."

Great – Any wine or vintage which is better than average.

Jeroboam – A huge bottle holding as much as four or five ordinary bottles. Named after a mighty Israelite.

Magnum – A large, heavy bottle twice as big as a normal-sized one, having great destructive potential. Must be grasped in both hands. Only to be drunk by professionals. .44 was a vintage of exceptional caliber.

Marc–A kind of brandy made by distilling the sediments, skins, and seeds. Pronounced "Maaarrh!" Known in Italy as *grappa*.

Moelleux–French for "very sweet." A difficult word to pronounce even before drinking some.

Mousseux–French for "fizzy." ("Mousse" is the head, or froth, on a glass of champagne or sparkling wine.)

MOG–Abbreviation for Matter Other than Grapes.

Oechsle–German way of measuring the ripeness of grapes. To talk about Oechsle numbers for wines, say, "Ah yes, 117 degrees Oechsle–phenomenal." It's the equivilent of using Koechel numbers for Mozart's works. It's proof that you're a true pro.

Ordinaire–Undistinguished.

Palate–The soft palate at the back of the mouth which is supposed to be an organ of taste. Actually the palate doesn't have much to do with taste at all. People with good palates are supposed to be skilled tasters. A good palate probably just helps you speak distinctly.

Pétillant–A sexy French word meaning "slightly sparkling."

Sekt–The German generic sparkling wine, drunk only by a small minority of wine drinkers who like their wines thin and acidy.

Sommelier–French for "wine steward."

Spritzig–A German word meaning "slightly sparkling," not nearly as sexy as *pétillant*.

Spumante – Italian word meaning "more than slightly sparkling."

Vin de table – Wine that will drink you under the table.

THE ULTIMATE
WINE BLUFF

Is your mind totally awash with superfluous information about vintages and varieties? Are you faced with a Monday night dinner party for your boss, who thinks he's a wine expert (no matter that he can't tell a Chardonnay from a Cabernet from Marquis d'Mogen David) and he told you this morning in doomsday tones how important he thinks it is for rising young executives to have a "Continental" image? And you've got nothing but a six-month-old half-bottle of Château Tony's Basement and a cold, dead-gray chicken leg in your refrigerator? Is that what's happening to you, Bunkie?

Don't go to pieces. Prepare! Here's how. First, declare with jaded ennui that European winemakers have become predictable and prosaic. "No surprises there," you say.

Such a blasphemous declaration will create a stunned silence, at least among those unsure of themselves in the rarified atmosphere of wine erudition (and that includes everyone you're likely to meet). Before anyone can gather themselves to counterattack, leap fearlessly into the breach like this:

"It's the small American wineries for me. They're the only ones anymore who'll *experiment!* They're the only ones who've managed to avoid genetic *suicide!* They've still got functioning *tastebuds!*" True? What do you care? Say it with enough élan and everyone will follow you around like intellectual puppies at Socrates' feet.

Now you choose some obscure winery in some obscure place—like Ohio or Kansas—to champion. Doesn't matter which—make one up if you like (after all, nobody will ever have been to such outposts), or use this one (and throw in lots of absolutely irrelevant facts).

- **Hermannhof** Boy, talk about innovative. That's in Missouri, of course.
- Restarted the thing in 1978. Had to dig out garbage from all the cellars, where the cretins started throwing it during Prohibition.
- Can't get it outside the state. (That way, you don't actually have to serve any at your party.)
- People came from Philadelphia, you know. Made their main street 10 feet wider than Market Street in Philly.
- Got the world's largest winehall.
- Come on. You believe that stuff about Midwest wineries always mixing their grapes with wine from other regions? Hah! Not *here.* They've even been experimenting with *viniferas.* Bury the vines in winter.

You get the idea. Be creative. Now you can serve (and enjoy) any wine you like, murmuring apologies all the while that you just couldn't get hold of Punxsutawney Pinot Penn or Wausau *Premier Cru.* And remember, if all else fails, as Harvey Barros said on *Making the Grade,* "It's *white* wine with Hershey Bars!"

Get Bluffer's Guides at your bookstore or use this order form to send for the copies you want. Send it with your check or money order to:

Centennial Press
Box 82087
Lincoln, NE 68501

Title	Quantity	$3.95 Each
Total Enclosed		

Name_____

Address_____

City _____

State_____ Zip_____